Vanishing Roadside America

Vanishing Roadside America

Warren H. Anderson

The University of Arizona Press

Tucson, Arizona

About the Artist/Author

WARREN H. ANDERSON's drawings have been featured in exhibitions at the Joseph Gross Gallery at the University of Arizona, the Phoenix Art Museum, the Ankrum Gallery in Los Angeles, and the El Paso Museum of Art. His work has also been seen in a nationally syndicated segment for CBS television. Dr. Anderson holds degrees from Western Illinois University and the State University of Iowa, as well as a Ph.D. from Stanford, and has taught in the University of Arizona Department of Art since 1956. He is the author of several articles and of a widely recognized text on art education, *Art Learning Situations in Elementary Education.*

Drawings in this book are from the following collections:
Air Cooled Waterfall in the Desert, Judd Kinne; *Beached Near Savannah,* Daumier Anderson; *The Sun Has Set for the Villa,* Dr. & Mrs. John V. Waddle; *The Closed Close Inn,* Courtesy of Joan Ankrum & Bill Challee, Los Angeles; *Twanggg . . . Don't Stay in the Cottage at the Rear!,* Doris & Corbyn Hamby; *The Nocturnal Monkeys of Phoenix,* Judd Kinne; *Swim Rose Swim,* Courtesy of Ankrum Gallery, Los Angeles; *Sprightly Pueblo Bandit Victim,* Janice S. Crebbs; *The Cowboys Always Smile,* Joseph H. Hirshhorn; *Great Head in a Coors Sky,* Jean C. Rush & William E. Martin; *Marie, Last of the Trucker Mothers,* Paul Benedict; *Empty Pot/Feathered Head,* Courtesy of Ankrum Gallery, Los Angeles; *Entwined Welcome in a Desert Sky,* Janice S. Crebbs; *Muy Rubio and Very Bright . . . at Night,* Joseph H. Hirshhorn; *Lovely Lady in the Desert Sky,* Courtesy of Joan Ankrum & Bill Challee, Los Angeles; *Rose About to Swim,* Vivian Cherry; *Rosedive,* Courtesy of Ankrum Gallery, Los Angeles; *Dislodged Navajo on Old El Cajon,* Brian & Mariane Anderson; *The Indians Seldom Smile,* Courtesy of Ankrum Gallery, Los Angeles; *Pegasus Departing from Sweetwater,* Linnea L. Anderson; *Benny's Drive-In Forever in Its 39th Year,* Audrey J. Anderson; *More of A Swamp Than A Gulf,* Mr. & Mrs. Harry C. Kinne Jr.; *Illumination of the Past,* Marcia & Richard Grand; *Restored Lone Star Radiance,* Private Collection; *Blue in the Georgia Rain,* Dr. & Mrs. William R. Noyes; *Secret Side Road Survivor,* Judd Kinne; *A Peeling Appealing Price,* Mr. & Mrs. Jack Furrier; *Fox Aglow in Westwood,* Terri Tilton; *Moderne Royalty on Wilshire,* Private Collection.

THE UNIVERSITY OF ARIZONA PRESS

This book was set in 11/12 V-I-P Kabel Book.

Library of Congress Cataloging in Publication Data

Anderson, Warren H.
    Vanishing roadside America.

    1. Commercial art — United States.   2. Signs and sign-boards — United States.   I. Title.
NC998.5.A1A5   741.973   81-11529
ISBN 0-8165-0746-5   AACR2
ISBN 0-8165-0754-6 (pbk.)

To Audrey
of the era
depicted here ...
except she's forever
in her 39th year

Contents

Foreword   James K. Ballinger   9
An Artist's Odyssey   11

Shapes and Letters as Signs of Mind   13
Moderne Pecos Pigeon Perch   14
Air Cooled Waterfall in the Desert   16
Full Up at a $1.25 a Nite   18
Indeed It Is   20

Ubiquitous Arrows Point the Way   23
The Linger Longer No Longer Lingers   24
Old Word in a New Buick Shape   26
Business Has Fallen Off   28
Early Space Age El Rancho   30
Beached Near Savannah   32
Rhode Service   34

Symbols as Shapes, Shapes as Symbols   37
Eatin' Up the Road   38
The Sun Has Set for the Villa   40
The Closed Close Inn   42
End of the (Rainbow)   44
Shamrock and U.S. 66   46

Pictured Words in Unison   49
Great Nozzle in the Sky   50
Twanggg . . . Don't Stay in the Cottage at the Rear!   52
Now Somewhat Less Than Regal   54
The Nocturnal Monkeys of Phoenix   56
Swim Rose Swim   58
Sprightly Pueblo Bandit Victim   60
Dallas Bronco . . . From Denver?   62
The Cowboys Always Smile   64
Great Head in a Coors Sky   66

Objects as Signs of Different Times   69
Haven for a Nite   70
Marie, Last of the Trucker Mothers   72

Holding the Fort in Phoenix 74
Empty Pot/Feathered Head 76

Signs with a Sense of Place 78
Peak Experience in Yuma 80
A Lost Mission for Motel El Don 82
Entwined Welcome in a Desert Sky 84
You Are Now Entering Texas 86

Independent Women, Indians, and Other Figures 89
My Place in Tulsa 90
Muy Rubio and Very Bright . . . at Night 92
Lovely Lady in the Desert Sky 94
Rose About to Swim 96
Rosedive 98
Dislodged Navajo on Old El Cajon 100
The Indians Seldom Smile 102
Post Civil War and World War II Optimism 104
       With Dolly Parton Sky

Bygone Corporate-But-Friendly Roadside Symbols 107
Pegasus Departing from Sweetwater 108
Benny's Drive-In Forever in Its 39th Year 110
Old Time Service in Cisco 112
More of A Swamp Than A Gulf 114
Illumination of the Past 116
Restored Lone Star Radiance 118
Homage to Edward Hopper 120
Blue in the Georgia Rain 122
Secret Side Road Survivor 124
Regal II, A Peeling Appealing Price 126
The Ghost of Ethyl 128

Continuing Attractions 131
Fox Aglow in Westwood 132
Moderne Royalty on Wilshire 134
Foxed Out in Tucson 136

All American Grilles Along the Way 139
Derelict DeSoto 140
Marilyn Monroe Caddy 142
Fin 144

Foreword

The subject of the drawings in this book is a small corner of the visual world available to us all. Warren Anderson selectively grasps the imagery of roadside signs constructed during the formative years of highway travel in the United States and transforms them into meaningful statements. In so doing, he does not merely provide a "snapshot" of the sign, but rather packs into one small image the sensation of a period in American history as we interpret it today.

Most of us living in today's highly technological society rarely take the time to really see the world around us. Of course, as we travel from home to work, or from city to city, we are constantly looking at everything in our field of vision; but, do we really *see*? To see is to do more than mentally record events and objects. To see is to both record and analyze those events and objects which are meaningful to our existence. Perhaps more than any other type of individual the artist truly sees our environment. He or she visually records data and, through creative analysis, can give a unique importance to otherwise ordinary things. The drawings reproduced here serve to lend a new significance to some roadside objects we may, until now, have taken for granted.

The 1930s and 1940s are rapidly becoming antique to many people. Anderson, with his colored pencil method of communication, makes a visual journey back into this past by subtly duplicating the effect of the high-chroma, linen textured bordered postcards of this period. The original postcards used a technique which cheaply reproduced the image as a type of "painting" with saturated, high-intensity colors. Anderson has succeeded in conveying the essence of these old cards while using colors more true to his subject.

The artist's careful study of motel, restaurant, gas station and other travelers' service signs reveals the impact of advertising art on the traveler of the thirties and forties. Bits and pieces of the signmaker's spirit are discovered and heightened through cropping of the image. Whether it be a shapely young woman diving into a motel swimming pool, the neon image of a gasoline pump nozzle, or a flashing arrow directing the driver to a restaurant entrance, these drawings force us to see and understand the intent of the sign recorded. Also, nostalgia itself can be seen as a subject of Anderson's eye. As we travel from San Diego to Savannah on U.S. Highway 80 and other old routes the style and flavor of Anderson's subjects speak of an individuality rare in today's world. The large majority of the establishments depicted in the drawings were small privately owned businesses. The Brandon Hotel, Rhodes' Auto Service and Warren's Fine Foods strike a different note from the expected Holiday Inns, Howard Johnson's and Midas Muffler Shops upon which today's traveler is so dependent. The unique intimacy communicated by individual signpainters of earlier eras has been replaced by the national image so highly prized by mammoth corporations of the seventies and eighties.

To label Anderson's work as being derived from the Pop Art movement of the 1960s would do it an injustice. Though Pop Art dealt with subjects we can term *roadside* in nature (cars, trailers, storefronts, etc.) and though some of its practitioners actually worked as signpainters, its driving force was an aesthetic of objects viewed from a neutral position and recorded in a detached fashion. Anderson's drawings are loaded with the intent of the artist to make a statement, easily understood in his subjects and titles.

Anderson's work can also be related to an artistic tradition which captured the imagination of many artists in the United States during the middle years of this century; that is, art about art. He does not bring forth the overt humor of Pop Art, or the obvious utilization of a historical masterpiece to be manipulated for an intended statement. Instead, it is the vernacular art of signmaking and advertising which becomes the focus of the artist's mind. It is here that Anderson concentrates artistic endeavor and it is here that his success lies. His perceptive eye takes us on a trip we can savor.

JAMES K. BALLINGER
Assistant Director, Chief Curator
Phoenix Art Museum

10

An Artist's Odyssey

The prismatic pencil drawings in this book are a response to a trend away from regionalism and individualism in advertising along the highways and streets of America. More than half of the signs depicted have vanished since the drawings were completed, and, in addition to my original intention to document other-era signs and objects along "Roadside America," I have come to feel a responsibility for the preservation of these rapidly disappearing vestiges of a vernacular American art form and a more leisurely mode of travel.

In the America of the 1920s the automobile began to be the common man's ship of discovery. During that time the federal government funded the completion of the long sought transcontinental Lincoln Highway and enacted other legislation that made voyages across this land more possible and pleasurable. These laws, combined with increased automobile production, led to the establishment of thousands of roadside services. Except for the period during World War II, these motels, gas stations and restaurants continued to proliferate for over three decades. Though the advertisements for these roadside businesses did contain elements of visual blight, they exhibited a spirit of optimism, security, and pride not found in today's slick and seemingly temporary images. These forms ranged in scale from individualistic, one-of-a-kind tourist court signs to sculpturesque gasoline pumps to strikingly designed porcelain-finish corporate logos. Of these, the tourist oriented signs were the most distinctly regional in character. But they all shared a style that clearly expressed the spirit of a new age of travel. The 35-mile-an-hour travelers knew where they were, both in terms of location and time.

Ironically, a later federal enactment contributed to the demise of these regional roadside art forms. The Federal Highway Act of 1956 authorized the 41,000 mile, four lane, limited access Interstate system. Much of this system was built primarily for national defense, not tourism. In the process of completing it many of the older major U.S. highways were either absorbed or bypassed. Accordingly, many of the small towns were also bypassed, and the localized travel-related businesses disappeared. These local enterprises have been replaced by large, nationally franchised establishments, usually located near Interstate interchanges far away from the former Main Street thoroughfares. The outcome has been that a national homogeneous highway community, lacking regional charm and individuality, has replaced the friendly network of motor courts and motels of the thirties, forties, and fifties. The intimacy and sense of uniqueness, so apparent in the old signs have all but vanished.

The drawings have been executed in the manner of the high-chroma, linen-textured, bordered postcards that were popular in the years when many of these roadside discoveries were in their apogee. The style of the drawings is therefore sympathetic with much of the era they represent.

Warren H. Anderson

Shapes and Letters as Signs of Mind

In looking at the objects documented by the drawings in this section, and in most of the sections that follow, some different approaches to reading can be tried. First, the actual shapes of the objects as defined by the outer edges can be read as significant in their own right. For example, the shapes of the 1920s are more angular. In the 1930s these contours were rounded and softened as streamlining came into vogue. Some streamlining lingered into the post-war years of the forties. Soon those shapes of the forties gave way to more complex outlines with an abundance of protrusions and occasional clutter.

Second, the shapes and consequent styles of the letters within these roadside objects are subjects for scrutiny. Many of the letters acquired rotund "cookie cutter" shapes. And third, both these outer and inner shapes say something of the times in which they were initially in use. They serve, unintentionally, as signs beyond their original function. They stand (or stood) as indexes into a way of life and, more specifically, a way of traveling that has all but vanished in much of the United States.

The drawings reproduced in this section are representative of styles typical of roadside signage in the 1920s, 1930s, and 1940s. In a sense they are pure shapes; unlike many of the objects depicted in subsequent sections, they contain no pictorial subject matter or symbols. But, though lacking in these visual statements they do say something. They are artifacts of another time and of a more subtle nature.

Moderne Pecos Pigeon Perch

Pecos, Texas

Not only this sign, but the entire hotel that supported it, has vanished since this drawing was completed. Perhaps the pigeons have survived. And, in one sense, the sign has survived — on this page and in the original drawing.

In terms of style and shape it was a curious object considering its location in the open spaces of west Texas. Its shape is derived from a style popularized in the 1920s as a result of an international design exposition held in Paris in 1925. The outer edges are in the shape of a squared-off angular waterfall motif. At the very bottom are some opposing angles and diamond shapes that graduated into zig-zag moderne when applied to larger structures. The cookie cutter letters, rotund and simplified, hint of the beginning of the streamlined era about to follow. Both the letters and the shape of the sign imply a rejection of Classical and Victorian ornateness. What decoration there is is more of a machine age ... merely echoing the crisp edges. So, way out west in formerly rugged Pecos there was a Parisian flair and a state of mind that said, "Let's be up to date." It is a statement full of vigor and confidence. In the '20s a system of national highways was designated and auto travel came into its own — for everyman. The Brandon, as the proud sign reveals, was open and ready for the influx. A Holiday Inn south of this site now serves that purpose. (11 7/8" x 7 7/8")

Air Cooled Waterfall in the Desert

Tucson, Arizona

If one could step into the past and, further, into some of the rooms of this mid-1930s tourist court, the furniture therein would most likely be in harmony with the softly rounded edges and letters of the sign. Waterfall styled headboards and dressers with round mirrors probably provided a visual echo of this sign. As to the comfort of the room on a hot summer night in the desert, the early traveler would have to realize that "air cooled" was not to be construed as air *conditioned*. In those days one would be lucky to have an evaporative swamp cooler working properly. When these coolers functioned they weren't bad at all — especially for $1.25 a night — or, apropos of the tendency to streamline nearly everything in that era, $1.25 a *nite*. (*11 7/8" x 7 7/8"*)

Full Up at a $1.25 a Nite

Tucson, Arizona

Like the price, the suspended shapes containing the streamlined words *no vacancy* and *steam heat* are pure 1930s. They are similar in character and spirit to the newly shaped trains of that era, the Burlington Zephyr and Rock Island Rocket. This sign, one of three that adorned the Sunset Villa Motel in South Tucson, has, in the meanwhile, streaked its way into oblivion.

Like many of these handcrafted, one-of-a-kind roadside statements this one is replete with artistry. Note how the rounded (streamlined) letter *A* echoes the left ends of the lower signs. Sheer harmony. The waterfall, placed horizontally above, arrests the speedy movement of those lower shapes. The peeling paint and dangling neon attested to its passing long before demolition occured. The Villa was bypassed by Interstate 10 long ago, subduing the optimism inherent in these not-so-pure shapes of that age. The price is factual. It was derived from a Conoco Tourguide published in 1937. Among the guests rumored to have stayed here is the notorious John Dillinger. One would think that he could have afforded something fancier and more expensive. (*11 5/8" x 7 5/8"*).

Indeed It Is

Georgia

Even the signs announcing this sign, and its related enterprise in a deeply forested region of Georgia, were fascinating. Miles from the actual Lonely Pines several introductory signs painted on now weathered horizontal wooden slats announced "private showers" and gasoline for 30.9 cents a gallon. Each was enveloped in vines and weeds alongside what was once a major U.S. highway, now bypassed by Interstate 16. These forlorn announcements proved to be precursors of the mood and state of this abandoned roadside business.

Well in front of some sturdy post-World War II red brick cottages this rusting sentinel stands. Its faded letters echo the derelict metal chairs stored neatly and symmetrically under the porches of the cottages. A dank gloom permeates the entire place — a perfect setting for a comeback of *The Twilight Zone*. Perhaps the late Rod Serling would have been intrigued by it. Sadly, its inherent optimism was not fulfilled. Even the attempt to keep up to date, as witnessed by the tacked on *T*, indicating the addition of air conditioning, did not save this roadside enterprise. Like so many of its post-war counterparts it was done in by four fast lanes that sped less leisurely motorists on their way far from what turned out to be the very, very Lonely Pines. Indeed. (*11 7/8" x 7 7/8"*)

Ubiquitous Arrows Point the Way

The emerging streamlined signs of the 1930s were merely symptomatic of the penchant for "laminar flow" that, more legitimately, found its way into automobile design in that same era. After all, cars do move! Also, thanks to the highway maintenance procedures decreed in 1925 by the National Highway Committee, roads were, like the cars that traversed them, becoming increasingly faster.

So, as attention-getting devices, the streamlined roadside signs were beginning to lag behind their stylistic counterparts on the highways. As a consequence an old idea from the early sign painters of Victorian times was resurrected in a somewhat modified form. Instead of a human hand with a pointing finger, the arrow was adapted as a means for informing the motorized traveler about accommodations and services. As a visual symbol it became the equivalent of a verbal shout. As time went by and travel increased both in speed and in proportion to population it became necessary to shout louder and louder. Thus these visual equivalents to attention-getting noise increased in both size and blatancy. A harbinger of a sort was lurking within and among the roadside objects.

The Linger Longer No Longer Lingers

Tucson, Arizona

As arrows go (swish?) this is a most subtle one — at least in the daytime. As to the shape of the sign, it is simple and only faintly suggestive of the 1930s. The wrap-around line at the center is of that streamlined era as are the three rounded off bars flanking the *LL* on top. The words *air cooled* and *cottages* further denote the time of origin. These characteristics, however, are overpowered by what only time and weather can produce; namely, a patina that in itself says so much. The patina provides a kind of benevolent dereliction. Aesthetically this aging texture has its attributes. Economically it indicated decline. This little sign and its once modern companions have all been blatantly bulldozed away. (*11 7/8" x 7 7/8"*)

Old Word in a New Buick Shape

Edwards, Mississippi

This weathered sign represents a fascinating amalgamation of both linguistic and visual styles. The word *court* dates back to highway travel of the 1920s. But the shape of the sign is in the manner of the more robust and dynamic automobile grilles that emerged in the late 1930s and early 1940s. There is a striking similarity between the shape of this sign and the grilles of the 1940 Buicks and De Sotos. This sign attemped to give a stamp of newness to some rather archaic shelters of and for the night. Air conditioning was apparently an afterthought.

A concession to the faster cars that cleaved the wind and sped down major U.S. highways was, however, assiduously built into this dual-era sign. The arrow clearly points to the back of a lot in this small Mississippi town where the courts awaited the weary motorist. It is, by contrast to those that follow, a rather diminutive arrow. Perhaps it made up for its size by flickering on and off at night. In essence, it tends to be an organic part of the design. (*11 7/8" x 7 7/8"*)

Business Has Fallen Off

West Monroe, Louisiana

American small town main streets were economically viable as long as an equilibrium between automobile and pedestrian traffic remained. Eventually, the car was allowed for, and main streets were extended into longer strips. Later still, after World War II, many of the major U.S. highways that originally passed through towns via the main drag were diverted to locations a few blocks away. This relocation soothed the time-bent traveler but not the deflated pockets of the local merchants. Thus the more dominant arrow built into this post-war sign. The stylistic shape of the sign is in keeping with the slanted shed designs that some of the service stations were acquiring at this time. The streamlined age was giving way to harder angles.

The condition of the sign at the time the drawing was made also bears a message of portent. The missing light bulbs imply an element of neglect. Ironically though, the broken neon which originally defined this hopeful arrow provided the metaphor incorporated into the title. The reason for all of this is based on a further bit of irony. The highway that circumvented main street has since been bypassed by an even more distant Interstate. This sign just seems to have given up, along with some of the original occupants of the area which it designated. An all too typical scene in America today. (11 7/8" x 7 7/8")

Early Space Age El Rancho

Lordsburg, New Mexico

Here is the zenith of arrow technology — wham-bang instead of twanggg-swish. This flashing, piercing shape signifies not only the drive-in entrance to the Hidalgo but also indicates that motorists were becoming numb from all of the increased highway signage competing for their attention. So, hit 'em on the head or between the eyes. Actually a hole was opened up on the highway side of this pre-motor age hotel so travelers could drive into the registration desk, sign in, and park in the courtyard. This arrow seems capable of making that very opening. The opposing angles and sharp edges of its companion shapes add to the overall dynamism (or chaos) of this precursor of the space age. In the meanwhile the protruding vigas provide a quiet grace left over from another time, a time before plastic TV letters. The empty light bulb sockets are no longer host to the flashing lights in accompaniment with the hyperactive arrow. Now only the bar remains open, preferably only to foot traffic and not to anyone driving in. Like so many of these highway vestiges that revealed a tendency to being up to date this sign has, paradoxically, become even more dated. It becomes one more artifact of a state of mind along the way. (11 7/8" x 7 7/8")

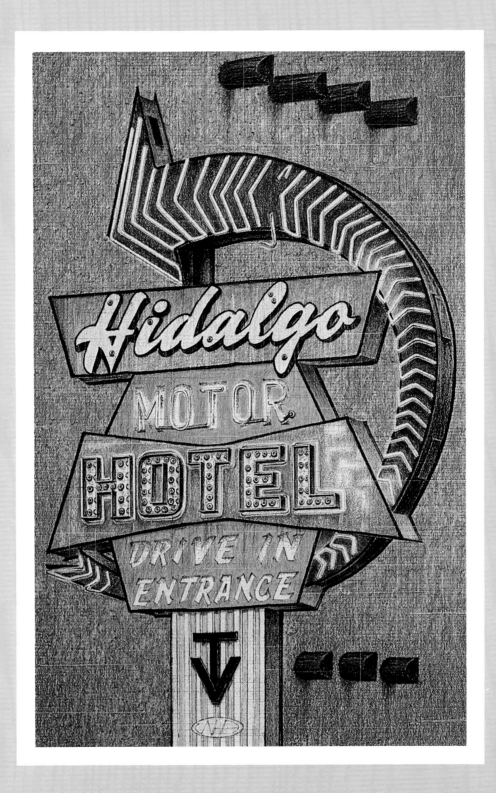

Beached Near Savannah

Savannah Beach, Georgia

Dwarfed by this huge shapey curvey turning arrow this diminutive member of the *Scolopacidae* family stands as a perky sentinel in front of a seashore motel only a few miles from the remains of old Fort Pulaski where Union Army sentinels held forth during much of the Civil War. Its real life counterparts scurry about the beach nearby at the very end, or beginning, of U.S. Highway 80. So, in terms of its proper habitat, this vernacular Audubon portrait of a sandpiper is right at home. In that sense he is not an environmental visual *non sequitur* as is the dislodged Navajo that stands at the western end of the same highway in San Diego.

As a guardian of light bulbs, the sandpiper apparently is not very successful. He more effectively stands guard for a disappearing breed of roadside art forms, a severely endangered species in its own right. (*11 7/8" x 7 7/8"*)

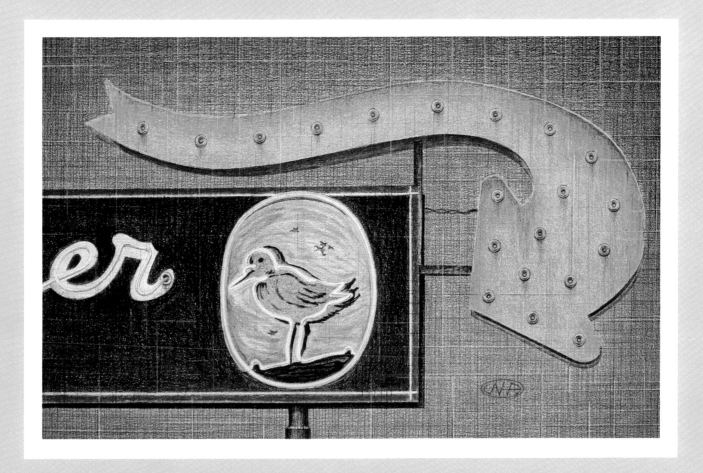

Rhode Service

Abilene, Texas

The swoop and sway of the interrelated shapes of the upper regions of this roadside statement are very similar to the body contours of the 1948 General Motors torpedo-style fastback cars. The styling of the sign brings to mind such post-war terms as *Fleetline*.

But even these wondrous, updated vehicles required attention and Mr. Rhodes seems peculiarly well suited to provide it. And, as evidenced by the tack-on mass-produced flashing arrow, the attention of the motorist was also needed. There is inherent in this odd combination of shapes a rather unfortunate hidden message; subtlety is in decreasing supply. And, akin to that possible message, perception is increasingly numbed. So, this interpretation implies a collision of styles and mentalities. The original yellow at the very top of the sign and in the middle strand of neon down below in the 1930s "three little lines" reveals some grace and a more subtle sensitivity. But, business must prevail ...
(*11 7/8" x 7 7/8"*)

Symbols as Shapes, Shapes as Symbols

Headed north on old Route 66 in a small Oklahoma town one is greeted by a bigger than life U.S. Route shield that contains the name "Hi-Way Cafe", in lieu of a route number. This is a classic example of a symbol (in this case a borrowed one) providing the actual shape, as well as a partial message, for the sign. Unlike the stylistic shapes which, intentionally or not, denote an era, these more abstract symbol-shapes are to an extent timeless, except when the symbol itself becomes outdated.

In other instances a borrowed symbol is used more indiscriminately than the one cited. Occasional Indian motifs are combined with names of businesses that bear no relation to those shapes. These may have been pioneers of what has since been called subliminal advertising. The shapes imply a sense of adventure beyond the mundane name of the business.

Not all of the shapes of the signs in this category are borrowed. Some are indeed original. They evolved out of a special problem of combining the name of a motel with a compatible shape in which to communicate it. Also, some symbols had to be invented because a handy repertoire from which to borrow did not exist.

In brief, the borrowing and inventing of symbols that become shapes (formats for the words) parallel what often happens in the so called fine arts. The history of art is replete with adaptations of icons. These signs related to travel are merely icons of a vernacular sort. They, like their more honorific ancestors, are continually shifting, changing, and, as the title of this book implies, disappearing.

Eatin' Up the Road

Bistrow, Oklahoma

The shield-shaped symbol that houses this message derives directly from that used to contain route numbers of all U.S. Highways. This borrowed symbolic shape stands alongside the noted U.S. 66. In 1925 the Committee on Interstate Highways decreed that there should be a nationally designated system of roads and that those running north and south should be assigned odd numbers while those running east and west should be labeled with even numbers. So, even with an impoverished sense of direction, the traveler along old 66 should realize that the road follows a somewhat east-west direction. Ironically, the colors of this sign (the original highway signs were black on white) are in keeping with those of the more recent Interstate highway shield which is a simplified abstraction of this old shape. The piercing arrow has many cousins elsewhere across the land and in this book. Taken literally, the title of the drawing commemorating this roadside vestige might make some sense. In terms of individuality, even though it is composed of a borrowed symbol, the sign makes good sense. It is not of the redundant corporate variety that so flavorlessly inundates the present-day roadscape of America. So here is one cheer for this aesthetic use of the red, white, and blue with a flavor of its own. (*11 7/8" x 7 7/8"*)

The Sun Has Set for the Villa

Tucson, Arizona

This radiant symbol accompanied by streamlined moderne letters no longer shines in the tiny enclave of
South Tucson. Well before its demise, the at once derelict yet fascinating patina had mellowed its former glow,
especially along the sunset bands of color at the top
of the sign. This is the third drawing derived from what
was left of that pleasant and homey Español styled clus-
ter of cottages. Only a clump of hardy oleanders and
a slowly crumbling concrete fountain attest to the former presence of what must have seemed like an
oasis to the desert traveler in the 1930s. That splendid intense turquoise-to-deep-blue sky still persists,
though there are days when its presence also seems in
doubt. (11 7/8" x 7 7/8")

The Closed Close Inn

South Tucson, Arizona

The outer edges that shape this sign bear some resemblance to a composite of a totem pole and a Hopi kachina. The zig-zag sunburst shapes also allude to another culture. However, there is a geographical gap of about 300 miles between Hopi land and the location of this motel.

The gap between the name of the business and the symbolic shape containing it is conceptually wide, as well. In all, however, an out west kind of warmth prevails. The contours of this 1930s sign also have some softness provided by the streamlined craze of that era and it shows a spirited vitality. Or at least it did. The entire enterprise has fallen to demolition. The addition of the letter *D* would have aptly foretold the destiny of the place. *(11 7/8" x 7 7/8")*

End of the ... (Rainbow)

Terrell, Texas

Nearly every town has one, along with a Dunes or Sands or Flamingo. Within this cliche name though there exists a variety of ways of visualizing a rainbow. The one depicted above is among the more abstract in shape and style. Obviously the spectrum beginning with red on top to violet on the bottom is disavowed. The arc doesn't quite make it either. The result is unique and refreshingly so. The uneven lower left is a dynamic complement to the wider upper right. Underneath it all is that prevailing reliance on streamlining. Thus the abstract rainbow as a unique shaper of this sign merges with the philosophy of the era; full speed ahead, while, of course, standing still. The primary colors are also more allied to the era than to the rainbow. Their vivid contrast is derived from the architecture of the 1933–34 Century of Progress World's Fair held in Chicago. "Tourist Court" at the verbal level is also contemporary with that event. But, as with many of these artifacts of roadside America the end may indeed be near, if not already here. (11 7/8" x 7 7/8")

Shamrock and U.S. 66

Shamrock, Texas

Up near the easternmost edge of the Texas Panhandle Interstate 40 buzzes by the little town of Shamrock. It also bypasses a stretch of U.S. 66 that formed the old tourist strip through this community. As this sign reveals, another route intersects 66. This intersection combined with the name of the town resulted in some rather original symbology. Though a bit garbled, the upper rounded section does attempt to communicate both crossroads and shamrock. Little did this sign know that it was also a harbinger of a future freeway intersection which, of course, contains a cloverleaf design as an interchange. May it rust in piece. (*11 5/8" x 7 5/8"*)

Pictured Words in Unison

The very letters that make up the words in these signs were once pictures, or, at least, pictographs. In a sense, then, the signs that reunite picture and word bring the process of written language back to its origins. The intentions are of course anything but that. The pictured words on these roadside statements are blatant, but often amusing, bits of reinforcement for an otherwise ordinary message.

The pictorial segments of these signs, like their word counterparts, range from the literal to the fantastic, depending on the nature and intended exotica of the service offered. In some cases the neon word could be extinguished (often the case at night) and the pictorial statement would articulate what was available quite on its own. On the other hand, in looking at some of these drawings minus the word the nature of the enterprise so symbolized would be not only vaguely defined but downright bizarre.

But perhaps the most effective communication to emerge from these other-era roadside vestiges transcends the original messages. In essence they show a spirit of fun and adventure—automobile travel as it was at least imagined to be in a less complex, less crowded, hassle-free time. Many of these pictorial signs were one-of-a-kind designs, executed by hand by artisans whose ranks have thinned. Many of these small scale intimate works have been replaced by huge, mass produced plastic signs that are the same from coast to coast, signalling the homogenization of American highways into one community.

Great Nozzle in the Sky

Sweetwater, Texas

The part of Texas in which this clear-cut message stands is more noted for its sweet oil than its water. When encountering this nicely balanced picture/word combination, one gets the feeling that an endless supply of gas oozes from the Permian Basin, directly up the pipe and out the nozzle into the gas tank. It is terse and to the point, especially at night. It must also have supplied a reassuring greeting to the traveler along the old highway. One of these signs was located at both the east and west approaches to the town. They were made for an independent dealer now, like so many, out of business. These once optimistic images, which implied a bountiful supply for all time, have become forlorn in their abandoned locations as a major Interstate highway swoops by them with, ironically, dwindling traffic. This sign stands now as more of an unintended metaphor than a functional object. (*11 7/8" x 7 7/8"*)

Twanggg (Don't Stay in the Cottage at the Rear!)

Mesa, Arizona

The name of this 1940s establishment is consistent with that of the street on which it is located, Apache Trail. Until recently that trail also bore the designation of U.S. Highway 80. Unlike many of his pictorial cousins, however, this native American is portrayed in a reasonably accurate manner, though he may be a bit chilly during the tourist season. But at least he isn't wearing a Plains Indian's feathered headdress, as is one of his neighbors a few blocks away (but many miles away with regard to the erroneous attire). One historical and cultural inaccuracy does persist though. At night the arrow becomes animated and takes on a trajectory toward the rear of the court. Western lore indicates that the various Apache tribes did not do that sort of thing after dark. So, perhaps the nocturnal residents of that cottage to the rear can relax a little after all. (11 7/8" x 7 7/8")

Now Somewhat Less Than Regal

Phoenix, Arizona

The king is represented here only by his crown and his title. At any rate, one may wonder how well kings did rest. Unrest may have been the rule. As to the use of the word *hotel*, that too may not make much sense in that these accommodations consist of twenty-five cottages, now apparently rented on a long-term basis and not to tourists. In the mid-thirties, as listed in Conoco's *Touraide*, these units rented for from $2.00 to $4.00 a night. And at that time they may even have appeared a bit more regal. This sign, with its 1920s heraldic symmetry, still exerts a modicum of dignity and decorum worthy of any court ... motor or otherwise. (*11 7/8" x 7 7/8"*)

The Nocturnal Monkeys of Phoenix

Phoenix, Arizona

Do two trees make a grove? There are some problems with words on this pictorial sign. Once a misspelling occurs in neon it is apparently too expensive to erase. But beyond these uses and abuses of language these words bear another message. Stylistically, that rounded *m* is a modernistic vestige from the thirties that carried over into the post World War II years. Cocanut (*sic*) Grove implies an element of pre-war swank. The three little lines, from that same period, have been modified by way of some waves. By contrast the monkeys are rather timeless. However, like many of the occupants of these pictured word signs, they are, along with the cocoanut palms, geographically out of sync. Neither of these fauna or flora resides in Phoenix — at night or any other time. As of now though these nocturnal scampering critters have yet to drop a cocanut (whoops!) (*11 7/8″ x 7 7/8″*)

Swim Rose Swim

Phoenix, Arizona

The pictorial rose offers the only symbolic consistency in this roadside beauty. The drawing shows the sign as viewed from the west. From this position, and thanks to the artist's editing, a person named Rose is encouraged to go for a swim. When viewed from the other side, the message is less clear. The disjointed lower word, when coupled with the upper word, suggests a "swim bowl." In reading the entire sign one realizes that is says simply, "Rosebowl Motel." And this is interesting in its own right. As exotic as Phoenix may have been to a traveler from more rigorous climes, it was evidently still lacking. *Rosebowl* was used to evoke the image of Pasadena which, at 350 more miles, was, in pre-Interstate times, another day's drive away. The implicit message is that it is supposedly better to be somewhere else when you are already somewhere else! In the meanwhile it's just nice to feast upon that one-of-a-kind, well-crafted neon rose. While doing so, seek the missing light bulb. *(11 7/8" x 7 7/8")*

Sprightly Pueblo Bandit Victim

Tucson, Arizona

In developing a regional drawing test called the S.A.T., the Saguaro Awareness Test, an art professor had observed that the majority of respondents draw this species of cactus with two upright arms as if viewed from the "front." Thus the term *bandit victim*. The inhabitant of this sign does have one arm a little lower than the other, thereby rescuing it from the typical kind of rendition. If it were not for the letter "O" however, that arm would probably be right up there with the other one. This same saguaro grows across the entire American West on all kinds of signs. In most instances they therefore become environmental non sequiturs in that they thrive only in Arizona and to the south in neighboring Sonora. This one is a bonafide native. The same level of accuracy does not apply to the use of the word *pueblo*. The present day pueblos are well to the north in New Mexico. The Spaniards did maintain one in Tucson in the 1700s. But they have since pulled out. One other observation; next to this pre-war pictorial sign is a newer one encased in a plain rectangle with only the same two words. Although it represents an attempt to improve it is also symptomatic of a blandness moving across the land. A few misplanted cacti might be preferable to that. (*11 7/8" x 7 7/8"*)

Dallas Bronco ... From Denver?

Dallas, Texas

This spirited Palomino, in a nearly identical stance, appears on many signs throughout the Southwest. He appears sufficiently frisky to warrant the title *Bronco*. Even though it has been awhile since the Denver Broncos played the Dallas Cowboys in the Superbowl this equine fellow may be looked upon as an intruder of sorts. But there are also plenty of cowboys to keep him in tow. For the present he provides this nicely designed sign with just the right amount of action to balance the two styles of lettering that refer to him and the nature of this roadside business along old U.S. 80 as it moves into Dallas from the west. (*11 7/8" x 7 7/8"*)

The Cowboys Always Smile

Big Spring, Texas

This uncool, pre-Marlboro-Man cowboy exudes 1940s optimism. Typical of his generation, his clean shaven face reveals a genuine down-home southwestern smile, on this sign and all of the others that bear a similar son of the west. And like so many of its counterparts that have been bypassed by the interstate highways this sign has since vanished. As it is portrayed in this drawing the word *vacancy* might have referred to the about to be vacated saddle should this stalwart fellow lose his grip. Instead the word proved to be an omen for the removal of the entire sign. Once again the drawing has become an act of preservation. One more bit of regionalism has slipped away. The nationally franchised motel a few miles down the road from this former enterprise bears the same name and sign as its corporate cousins in New Jersey and elsewhere. In that he is not an urban cowboy it is unlikely that this pardner would be at home there or in any other place differing from this range. Little did he know that in tipping his hat he was saying good-bye rather than hello. (*11 7/8" x 7 7/8"*)

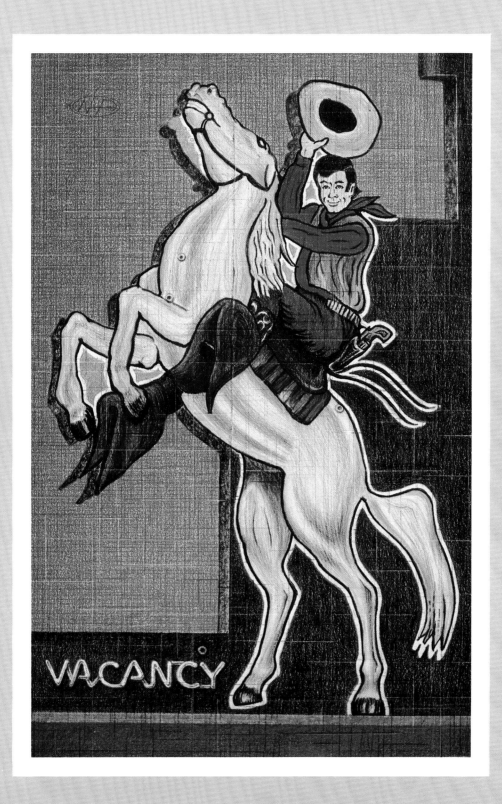

Great Head in a Coors Sky

Tucson, Arizona

Should the swamp coolers in some of the nearby ghost motels of the 1930s fail to function some respite might be available from the ingredients portrayed in this sky-high singular still life. A probable date for this vernacular object would be circa 1948 B.S.P. — before six packs. As with most of the objects interpreted in these roadside drawings this one appeals to those with wheels. Although it is on a pre-interstate scale, being somewhat intimate and inviting, it is perched on high. Its head is in the clouds. And the word *drive* implies that one just doesn't stroll in for a sip. *Inn* is misleading because no overnight accomodations exist. It represents just one more bit of linguistic license in conjunction with the motor age. It is also of interest to note which item on the menu was selected for portrayal to lure the motorist "inn." Somehow chicken and shrimp do not lend themselves to this genre of highway still life painting. Besides, that high altitude head of beer takes on certain cloud-like characteristics, especially against the intense blue of this rather typical Arizona sky. Doubly refreshing. *(11 7/8" x 7 7/8")*

Objects as Signs of Different Times

In vernacular architecture commercial buildings that are in the shape of an object other than a building, such as the original Brown Derby Restaurant in Los Angeles, are referred to as *ducks*. The term originated from a building in that fowl shape located on Long Island. The counterparts to these joyous architectural wonders also exist on a smaller scale, along American highways, in the form of signs that are in the shape of an object that relates to the enterprise so advertised.

Invariably these objects-as-signs are one of a kind, hand crafted near the region of installation and display, and foremost among the vanishing breed of vernacular art. As signage their historical roots are deep. They date back to medieval times when, among a large illiterate populace, signs communicated available services predominantly through pictorial shapes — a shoe for a shoemaker and so forth. Enlarged to the faster moving vehicular traffic demands of the forties and fifties, these modern day counterparts exhibit an appropriate increase in scale. And they do contain words, also on a fairly large scale. In a sense the words are redundant. Occasionally, though, they clear up any final ambiguity that may exist about the nature of the services offered at a particular stop for the travelers whether they be motorists, trailer folk, or truckdrivers — or Indians looking for a lodge.

Haven for a Nite

Holtville, California

Where else but in southern California would one expect to find such a splendid amalgamation of moderne and Islamic lettering and place names amid an appropriate technicolor sky. The spelling of night in *overnite* further denotes the era in which this object-shaped sign was made. The 1940s style of the trailer also serves as a dating device. It, the sign, and the trailer park have vanished. A few nearby date palms provide a visual echo of what was once a welcome oasis for motorized nomads on the way to the shrine of Los Angeles. (*11 5/8" x 7 5/8"*)

Marie, Last of the Trucker Mothers

Benson, Arizona

This object-as-a-sign is nearly as large as the truck from which it was derived. Its size, however, fits in nicely with the wide open skies of southern Arizona. The blue hue of that same sky also provides a color complement to the weathered orange that is unique to this region.

As the drawing implies, this particular symbol is parked at a rather high altitude. This heavenly status may account for its longevity. The business, in fact the building itself, which this truck identifies, has fallen into ruin. Meanwhile the symbol that corresponded to the reality underneath it has outlasted that which it symbolized. Very much like the history of art. And, this vernacular exemplar of *ars longa* has also outwitted the typically dimwitted vandals that attack such splendors. (*11 7/8" x 7 7/8"*)

Holding the Fort in Phoenix

Phoenix, Arizona

Phoenix? Not San Antonio? Exactly. Unlike its namesake, which has survived for a century or so, this establishment is already extinct. So is John Wayne, who may have served as the prototype for the armed figures appearing in the tiny painted apertures. They held this fort from the thirties until it fell in the seventies. Like some of its neighbors along Van Buren Avenue it allowed the traveler to imagine that he was somewhere else should Phoenix not be sufficiently exotic in its own right. Nearby is the Rosebowl, a Pasadena transplant, and the Liberty, with its Statue borrowed from an even more distant locale. While the fort shape at the top of the sign bears some resemblance to its eighteenth-century Texas counterpart, the style of lettering below shifts to the streamlined era. After all, an air conditioned fort is much easier to defend ... especially during a Phoenix summer. *(11 7/8" x 7 7/8")*

Empty Pot/Feathered Head

Mesa, Arizona

Here there are two objects for the price of one. And what objects they are! The Pueblo-style pot, miles removed from its place of origin, provides good news for the weary traveler only when it is empty; quite the opposite of any meaning associated with the actual function of its real-life counterpart. An emptiness of a more cerebral kind may be attributed to the association of a Plains Indian headdress with those of any of the thirty or more tribes that reside in Arizona. But anthropology this sign ain't. Instead it is a very artistic pictorial object that lets the traveler experience the sense of adventure that he seeks. It's fun, it's bright, and it offers something unavailable in the more distant Pueblo country. Those kivas are not air conditioned. (11 7/8″ x 7 7/8″)

Signs with a Sense of Place

Many of the older roadside signs had, in addition to handcrafted figures and letters, a genuine hand-painted scene. In most instances the scenes served only as a background for the major, neon-trimmed figure.

As with mis-headdressed Indians and other visual incongruities, certain flaws concerning flora occured, along with some geological inaccuracies. It is these inaccuracies, however, that become rather accurate indicators of a state of mind that accompanied the entire travel package process. In the thirties travelers were often literally escaping something, usually a bad economic situation. After World War II there was an escape into some new freedoms — no more duty to the military and plenty of gas and food. Travel to faraway places on a voluntary basis became a sudden reality. The signs of these times promised the fulfillment of the desire to be someplace else — on one's own terms for a change. In fact, they very often let the traveler know, minus a few facts, where he wanted to be. This was more important than always knowing exactly where he was. After all, travel in the early post-World War II years, when these signs flourished, was more for fun than function. These few remaining roadside vestiges are a tribute to and a celebration of those halcyon days.

Peak Experience in Yuma

Yuma, Arizona

If one is at all familiar with the climate and terrain of Yuma, Arizona, this scenic sign will be appreciated as a classic environmental visual non sequitur. There are mountains nearby, but they are low and brown, chocolate to be exact. No white topping ever appears on their peaks. As for Yuma itself, it's nearly always hot. Legend has it that soldiers stationed at Fort Yuma in the 19th century, would find it necessary to take a blanket with them if, in the afterlife, they were condemned to hell.

This roadside bit of surrealism offers pines instead of palms for the travelers of the pre-auto air conditioning era. Thus this scene inadvertently reveals a true sense of place. When in Yuma, it is essential to cool it. It's also a nice visual pun. There is great delight for the eye and mind in this scenic wonder, providing one can over- look the absence of the apostrophe. Poetic license is hereby extended to the artisans of roadside America. (11 7/8" x 7 7/8")

A Lost Mission for Motel El Don

Banning, California

This once proud landowner, stripped bare of his neon, seems to be surveying his rather desolate realm as if in search of lodgers for the night. This figure in a scene stands along old Highway 99 well east of Los Angeles. Interstate 10 zooms by a few yards south of old El Don. Just hanging on to his domain by way of some weekly or monthly rate occupants, he gazes fixedly on a scene formerly uninterrupted by the vast eight lane streak of concrete nearby. The horse, as if in anticipation of this intrusion, seems to have recoiled in advance. It was a lovely scene. Like many of these portrayals of place there is, however, a minor inaccuracy. Those multi-armed Saguaro cacti do not grow in California. Their habitat ceases a few miles east of the Colorado River over in Arizona. (11 5/8" x 7 5/8")

Entwined Welcome in a Desert Sky

El Paso, Texas

Here is the ultimate in lasso art. This trickster with the rope excels at rounding up tourists rather than critters. He shares with his southwestern compadres that clean-cut pleasant face. The scene in which this wondrous use of rope takes place is "genuine western" in appearance, though the plants are a bit ambiguous. They reside as species somewhere between sagebrush and prickly pear. Perhaps they represent a hybrid. But nothing is impossible after that feat of spelling in mid-air with the lasso. Sadly this art of writing and drawing in neon is in decline. It seems less and less possible to produce the neon pictorial sign in its own right. There is some indication that there is less than one tenth of the number of these neon artisans than in the 1920s. This paucity of skill is also reflected in the maintenance, or lack of it, of the signs. The slow disappearance of this art form is a result of many influences. Chief among these are zoning laws and an energy-saving consciousness. The end result may be a roadside America that reveals and commemorates little of a sense of place. (*11 7/8" x 7 7/8"*)

You Are Now Entering Texas

El Paso, Texas

. . . or leaving it if westbound. Either way the prickly pear cacti, which really do grow in this area, seem to smile right along with the friendly cowpoke. These roadside cowboys invariably smile. They do not possess the psuedo cool of the present day billboard breed. The terrain too is authentic. It provides a sense of place in keeping with this region. Those popcorn clouds do not, however, correspond to the gently floating ones in the actual west Texas sky. They do (kind of) belong with the impossibly peppy lasso though.

The metamorphosis this roadside attraction has undergone is of further interest. It reveals the enthusiastic enterpriser's attempt to keep up to date. This outlook emerged in the 1930s and picked up again just after World War II. It comes forth mainly in the add-ons. The *swimming pool* addition harmonizes with the boxed neon letters of the original upper area. A decline in craftsmanship and élan had occurred by the time *TV* and *AIR* were added. The letters designating these additions are of the cheaper, easy to hang expedient style. They bespeak a less artful era. If their colors are taken literally one can infer that the TV is black and white while the air gushes forth in color. That often repainted scene some- how prevails as an element of stability, even though something of the original shapes and colors is lost in the re-do process. The scene not only shows a sense of place but a state of mind that contrasts vividly with the impersonal hang-on plastic letters that interrupt in more ways than one. (*11 7/8" x 7 7/8"*)

Independent Women, Indians, and Other Figures

This particular "signdrome" often relies on a singular human figure, well separated from the accompanying words, to catch the eye. Viewed separately, as in some of the following drawings, these figures take on an independent existence of their own. Stylistically, they resemble blown up comic strip characters, with a little archaic Greek stiffness and neo-primitivism thrown in. They do not give the illusion of renaissance roundness. Flatness prevails.

In addition to the flat painting style, these figures are also composed of four flat sides. The inner surfaces of smooth tin may or may not be painted in correspondence to the exposed surfaces that constitute the shape of the figure. Thus these roadside inhabitants seldom become truly convincing sculpture. They do, however, possess a certain personality. They are usually hand crafted and one of a kind. Moreover, they are most often done from memory—not from posed models—and most memory drawings are based on certain conventions within a culture. This reliance on conventions results in a kind of stereotype, often of a sexual or racial nature. Thus the females are usually shown as sweetly standardized and buxom. The Indians appear glum and downtrodden.

Once again these exemplars of roadside vernacular art serve as inadvertent social and historical documents. The attitudes latent within them are not always flattering to our culture at large. Artistically though these rapidly vanishing independent figures, their colors softened by time and weather, helped to create a roadside gallery that was a little more individual and a little less humdrum. Better this than an ever increasing homogeneous land of the bland.

My Place in Tulsa

Tulsa, Oklahoma

This dutiful damsel provides an artistic counterpoint to the more ordinary words and competing arrow. Her hair styling and general demeanor place her in the late 1940s. It should be made clear, in case the drawing isn't, that those are rust spots, not stains, on that otherwise crisp white uniform. As mentioned, there is a sense of service implied in this independent figure. Along with this good old fashioned dedication and courtesy it also appears that the food will arrive to the customer piping hot. Hur-rah! Long may she serve, in Tulsa and in other similar stops for the traveler across the land. (*11 5/8" x 7 5/8"*)

Muy Rubio and Very Bright . . . at Night

Los Angeles, California

This very independent lady reigns in Los Angeles in a different capacity from those figures depicted in most of these postcard drawings. She signifies an entertainment spot. She is more streetside than roadside but nonetheless represents a diminishing vernacular art form. Her stacked up blonde hair-do is reminiscent of that worn by the chorus girls in 1930s burlesque shows, and later in movie musicals. The then skimpy costume, clinging seductively, seems modest nowadays. In all it is a very scintillating Hollywood-type production. It is only appropriate that she continues to glow in Los Angeles, the city that had the first neon sign in the U.S.A. That sign was installed at the Earle C. Anthony Packard dealership in 1923. Perhaps this pretty gal rode in one of the later models — but not too much later. (*11 5/8" x 7 5/8"*)

Lovely Lady in the Desert Sky

Holtville, California

Perched high in the sky above Main Street in the desert town of Holtville, about to dive into a cool, watery oasis, is this lovely lady from the past. Her singularity dominates the monotony of two varying sized rectangles containing the message. Her modest one piece bathing suit is contemporary with the language in the sign—*Motor Inn* rather than *motel*.

Forever caught in her mid-air dive, she once served as a beckoning refreshing symbol for the parched, overheated, pre-air conditioned automobile traveler. Today's cool encapsulated motorist, traveling along Interstate 10 well south of Holtville, is deprived of her countenance. Though she is unique in execution and placement she does have many cousins across the land. But as with the aquamaids of the old, carefully choreographed movies, their performances have nearly ceased. (*11 7/8" x 7 7/8"*)

Rose About to Swim

Mesa, Arizona

This young lady is a member of a team that performs on thousands of signs throughout the country. In the daytime there are several stationary Roses poised well up in the sky on this tall animated specimen. At night each one appears intermittently and in sequence to provide the traveler with a most exquisite diving exhibition. This stellar Olympic performance is the result of a fine combination of art and technology. The accomplishments of the neon artisan are apparent. The success of the nighttime animation, however, depends on a consistent electrical current that flows smoothly enough to make neon function properly. So this independent woman is clearly a product of our technological era ... an era which abounds in interdependence. (11 7/8" x 7 7/8")

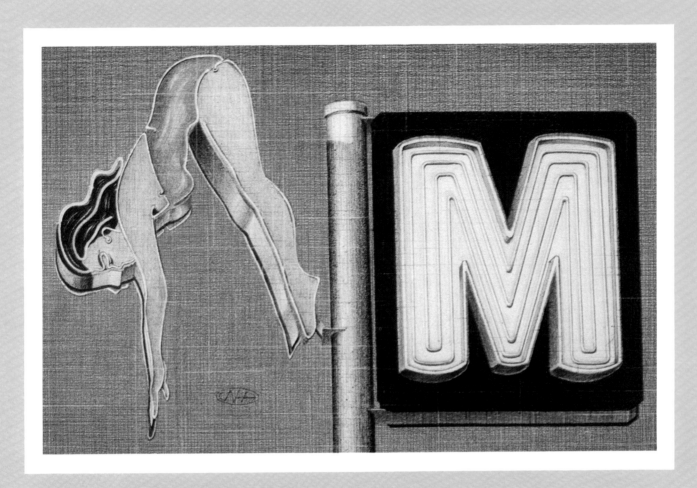

Rosedive

Mesa, Arizona

If the various electrical circuits are cutting in and out properly, Rose, in cooperation with her other selves, will complete a successful dive. Unfortunately this nocturnal descent culminates on a disastrous note. She is headed not into an inviting swimming pool but instead onto a hard surface near the road. At this rate she may become a part of obliterated roadside America. She must, however, be of Olympic calibre in that she completes dozens of dives each night. *(11 7/8" x 7 7/8")*

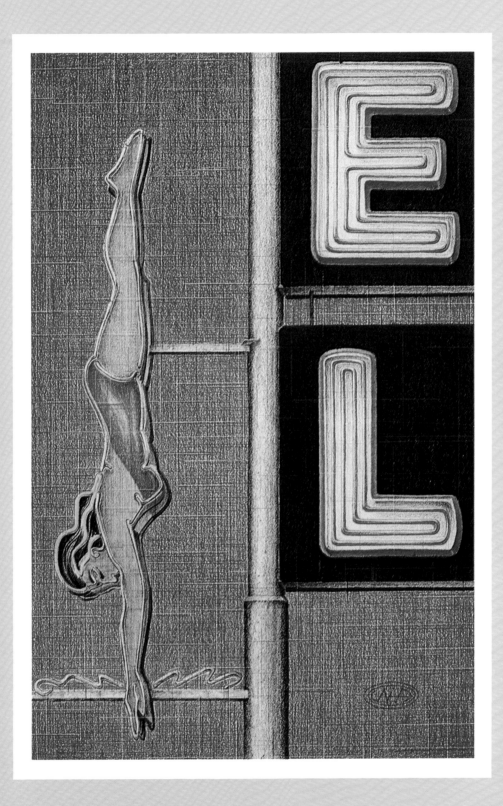

Dislodged Navajo Along Old El Cajon

San Diego, California

Highway maps from the thirties and forties indicate that El Cajon Boulevard in San Diego was once a major tourist route. It was, in fact, the western terminus of former U.S. Highway 80. This stretch has been bypassed by Interstate 8 and many of the modern corporate giants of the travel industry are located along a stretch of it known as Motel Circle.

Meanwhile, some of the older tourist establishments survive. Among those is the one identified by this wayward drum beater from Arizona. He must be quite chilly as he flails away in the cool gray sea air — especially since, like so many of his animated neon brethren, he works only at night. The drum playing now appears to be somewhat off beat though. And, for a Navajo, the Plains headdress too is out of sync. Not too far from this sign there is a life-size wigwam to keep the headdress company. So, neither the headgear nor the abode of the Navajo has been adhered to here in San Diego. A sense of adventure again surpasses anthropological fact. But this former tourist strip still provides us with some unintended cultural artifacts that allow us a glimpse into another era of travel in America. This specific visual non sequitur displays a verve that is absent in the various motel districts along the homogeneous interstates. (*11 7/8" x 7 7/8"*)

The Indians Seldom Smile

Big Spring, Texas

The inspiration for this independent figure comes from a very popular reproduction that adorned many a parlor wall in the 1930s. That reproduction, in turn, was derived from a sculpture entitled, "The End of the Trail." Ironically, this three dimensional roadside statement has followed a long trail back to its spatial ancestry.

If the cowboys are always smiling on these regional art forms it follows that the Indians seldom are. A certain unintended social truth again emerges from this native symbology in front of the Trail's End Motel. The historical evidence indicates that most Indians had remarkably little to smile about as the frontier pushed through this part of the country. But now a frontier of a different sort has made its mark. The Interstate has bypassed the old highway and this motel has met the end of its trail. The sign most aptly symbolizes the status of the place. Just down the road a motel sign containing a typical smiling cowboy has already vanished. His neon adversary barely survives.

The brickwork beneath the forlorn rider forms a planter, a curious post-war artifact that promises to become a ubiquitous ruin from a recent past—as well as a repository for objects other than plants. Both the independent figure and the brickwork reveal a level of craftsmanship that has diminished. The pinto takes on a painterly quality as a result of time and weather, and the many hands that have retouched the original. These restorers often have difficulty following the intentions of their more talented predecessors. A funny unity results. (11 7/8" x 7 7/8")

Post Civil War and World War II
Optimism with Dolly Parton Sky

Montgomery, Alabama

Here is an exemplar, though slightly cartoonish, of regionalism with pride. This roadside colonel lets travelers know exactly where they are. And they know they are not in South Dakota. He stands along U.S. 80 not far from the White House of the Confederacy. The colonel is standing on a flagstone planter, a post-WW II artifact complete with a rakish angle projected toward the road. These obligatory planters were the craze in living room entryways and as gas station exterior decoration in the late forties. Though born of a kind of aesthetic impulse, many of these became repositories of debris, rather than of plant life. The shape of the sign is of an incipient space-age classic style. On a smaller scale it might be considered a do-dad. Linguistically, the words *hotel* and *court* linger on, as does this stalwart fellow, clearly at home in his territory. (*11 7/8" x 7 7/8"*)

Bygone Corporate-But-Friendly Roadside Symbols

A few years ago Conoco changed its symbol, an upside down triangle, to a horizontal rectangle with rounded corners and softer letters. Consumer research had indicated that the former symbol was perceived by the public as unfriendly. In the last few decades many of the familiar corporate symbols have been redesigned. Nearly all of the newer symbols have arrived at an easy-to-see-and-grasp sleekness, with more of a technological quality than a human touch about it.

There is literally a new dimension to these roadside corporate visualizations. They have assumed a much larger scale than their predecessors. One letter on an Interstate Exxon sign is larger than an entire oldtime porcelain Shell symbol. There is less of a tactile quality to the newer designs. They are out of reach. Even the gasoline is no longer visible in the pumps. Only numbers in a computer-like case spin about, the price tabulation a blur. The gallons move more slowly.

The postcard drawings immediately following celebrate a time when even professionally produced corporate roadside objects appeared on a more intimate scale. Even though they were not one of a kind they had a friendly keeping-in-touch quality about them. They were not remote and out of scale.

107

Pegasus Departing from Sweetwater

Sweetwater, Texas

The predecessor to Mobil's soaring equine symbol was the Socony-Vacuum Gargoyle. Pegasus took over in the thirties. He definitely has more appeal emotionally, and perhaps, logically. After all the word *gas* is embedded in his name. Though a corporate symbol, this particular breed is presented on a more intimate scale and in a more durable material than many of its huge, modern Interstate rivals. The porcelain surface is embellished with finely detailed neon, materials that glistened by both day and night. The angle at which this Pegasus is depicted reveals something of his free-spirited character. This same carefree feeling was epitomized in an ad published by Mobil in a 1939 *Life* magazine. The ad shows a couple zoomin' along in a convertible. The woman is driving, her hair blowing, and the young man is smiling, as both, buoyant and forever youthful, continue on the "flight."

This particular Pegasus, however, no longer soars. He is probably earthbound in some collector's stable. And of course the commodity he identifies is diminishing each day. His departure may be one more omen for automobile travelers in this land. It might also be of interest to wonder how the couple in the 1939 ad has changed. May their youthful spirits drive on with the image of this red steed ... and may they never run out of gas on their timeless journey. (*11 7/8" x 7 7/8"*)

Benny's Drive In, Forever in Its 39th Year

Monterey Park, California

This bright intimate small-scale 1940s corporate sign is fairly near two towns whose place names Jack Benny liked to kid about—Azusa and Cucamonga. Though Jack had nothing to do with this enterprise, there is something enduring and memorable about its little sign. First, the Art Nouveau style lettering in the trade name has been around since the turn of this century. It is still beautiful. Second, the proprietor's name is in neon. This in itself implies stability. Contrast this element of commitment to the easily removable stick-on plastic letters of today. The latter imply instant bankruptcy. The reds and greens are also corporate colors. Again, time softens these. In its entirety, this old sign bespeaks another set of values and another time. May it glow in the pearly Los Angeles sky incessantly! *(11 5/8" x 7 5/8")*

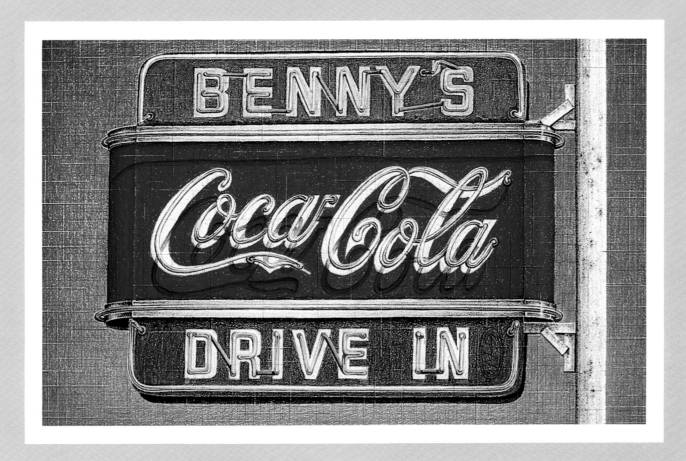

Old Time Service in Cisco

Cisco, Texas

A close inspection of the corporate sign in this drawing will reveal some small chips in the surface. Note further an irregular white rim between the rusted inner surface of the chips and the gleaming outer finish. This minute visual statement subtly communicates the kind of material used in its production; namely, porcelain. Again, they "don't make 'em like that any more." The luminosity of color provided by the porcelain finish has endured for over forty years. Even the chips, as long as they are kept to a minimum, add character to it. Unfortunately too many of these older small scale signs have fallen victim to misguided shootists. This particular survivor is well within the city limits, thus its presence.

The primary colors are right out of the 1930s. They provide a bright, strong contrast. With regard to the simplified lettering, note that *Chrysler*, in addition to being on top, is composed of sharp, hard-edged letters, whereas *Plymouth* is down below and softly rounded. Supposedly one is classier than the other. In the meanwhile, this intimate sign with its rather enthusiastic mood hangs on. (*11 5/8" x 7 5/8"*)

More of a Swamp than a Gulf

Georgia

In that this sign is located at the edge of a vine-entangled swamp, it makes, by way of its brand name, a neat parody on itself. Though this is a corporate symbol its small scale coupled with the hand-lettered town name qualifies it as being much friendlier than its latter-day gargantuan plastic descendants that loom over the Interstate interchanges. No embracing vines will grow over those high-in-the-sky giants.

This sign also has some material benefits. It is finished in porcelain which has long-since become a rarity. The style of the lettering fixes its date of birth somewhere in the late 1930s and the complementary colors make it highly visible even though it is only about four feet wide. Its ornate metal holder with its fancy curliques harks back to Victorian times. Somehow this mixture of styles and the encroachment of the natural environment all work in harmony to produce a roadside visual statement that is most unique. It is truly complementary—to the landscape and to its era of origin. (*11 7/8" x 7 7/8"*)

Illumination of the Past

Macon, Georgia

U.S. Highway 80, which still goes through the downtown area of Macon, gives the present-day motorist a
feeling of what it was like to travel in pre-Interstate days.
The old parking garage to which this sign is attached is
across the street from a hotel that it has apparently
served for a few decades. It is even possible that this
building was a livery stable prior to the advent of automobile travel, because the fixture to which the globe
is attached is very ornate late Victorian. The globe was
added in the 1930s and its soft nocturnal glow still offers
a friendly reassurance to the traveler that some kind of
service is available. In spite of their aesthetic differences,
the two elements seem meant for each other and their
partnership has endured. (*11 7/8" x 7 7/8"*)

Restored Lone Star Radiance

Douglas, Arizona

The globe for this roadside beacon no longer exists. Art has come to the rescue, though, by way of memory and imagination, and it glows once again. The pump itself is still poised where it has always been. It was manufactured by the Tokheim Pump Company of Thor, Iowa, in 1938. Tokheim means *take home* in Norwegian. So here we have a Viking standing steadfast among Russian thistle near an old shed in the Southern Arizona desert and linking us to another time. (*11 7/8" x 7 7/8"*)

Homage to Edward Hopper

Georgia

This roadside sentinel takes on a luminescent glow when seen in the rain. The drawing tries to reveal that quality. The red pump with its beckoning friendly globe against a dark sky is somewhat reminiscent of a 1940 painting by Edward Hopper tersely entitled, "Gas."

The globe atop this pump is an increasingly rare survivor. By the late fifties most that were still intact were either vandalized or collected. Their absence represents one less note of warmth for the traveler. In a sense these friendly beacons were comparable to a light left on in the window at home for whomever might be away.

As for the pump itself, the little transparent hemisphere to the left displayed what kind of gasoline you were getting. This kind of direct experience has become scarcer, along with the product being dispensed. Even the contents of this roadside object had a friendlier name, far more personal than premium or super. Where has Ethyl gone? (11 7/8" x 7 7/8")

Blue in the Georgia Rain

Brooklet, Georgia

This drawing depicts two old Vikings deep in the Georgia woods. Log construction, originally developed to protect against the long Scandinavian winters, seems to have come full circle when seen as backdrop for this old Tokheim pump.

A harmony of a more aesthetic nature is also seen in this drawing. The gentle rain bathing the surface of this streamlined pump allows the complementary orange and blue to glisten in a glowing partnership. As old cars seem to run better when it rains, this roadside survivor looks better … despite the rust so prevalent in this climate. Somehow even that rust seems at one with both the aesthetic and cultural aspects embodied in this postcard drawing. (11 7/8" x 7 7/8")

Secret Side Road Survivor

Georgia

This mid-1930s pump is virtually a miniature skyscraper in styling. Its free flowing waterfall and streamlining effects are in the spirit of an era which celebrated technology and the machine. Times were hard but this faith in becoming modern provided an impetus for a recovery of both the pocketbook and the psyche. There is no depression evident in this proud and dynamic roadside object. The fact that it still survives is a further indication of the state of mind of the period in which it originated. It's durable. Most goods of that time were, because a sense of craftsmanship and care still prevailed.

The rather realistic replica of the shell atop this modern wonder is clearly of an even earlier time. It seems ornate and old fashioned when compared to its support, and has elements of grace and character, qualities which have become scarce. Somehow this globe, despite its contrasting character, harmonizes with the pump. That price per gallon would certainly seem more harmonious. But it is only through art that time and prices can be rolled back. Thus this drawing. *(11 7/8" x 7 7/8")*

Regal II, A Peeling Appealing Price

Tucson, Arizona

In the field of environmental aesthetics there is a theory that says a man-made structure must become a ruin before it is considered to be worthy of preservation. By the time a structure has arrived at a state of dereliction, however, it is at best a candidate for restoration. Most likely such man-made objects fall way, literally, to demolition. In the long run this prevents overcrowding within our landscape. On the other hand the demolition of the past also destroys a kind of visual continuity that we all need in order to feel at home in an environment.

The sign depicted in this drawing, along with the station that it advertised, is gone. And so are those prices. Perhaps the economic tie-in makes this object even more appealing. As it stands now, only in this drawing of course, it is another document of an irrecoverable set of circumstances with regard to travel in America. (11 5/8" x 7 5/8")

The Ghost of Ethyl

Texas Panhandle

The spirit of technology so prevalent in the industrial designs of the 1930s is evident in this old pump. Contours similar to these may also be found in its roadhouse cousin of the same era, the jukebox. Moreover, these contours echo a turn-of-the-century grace. The inherent structure is further enhanced in a way never intended by layers of paint and varying corporate decals that have been modified by time and weather. The result is a patina that gives a rather ethereal mood to this roadside object. The setting too contributes to this mood. The pump is secluded under a shady wooden structure that creaks when the winds of the Texas Panhandle blow forth. In all this ghostly configuration are embodied two rapidly vanishing characteristics from the past ... namely, grace and ethyl. Or is that Grace and Ethyl? Either way, neither is present in the contemporary counterparts of this friendly roadside dispenser. Nowadays the customer does not even have the opportunity to see the gasoline spinning in the little amber window. Instead he is confronted with the rapidly blurred numbers of the "cents [or dollars] per gallon." Hardly a graceful experience. Goodbye to Ethyl as well. (11 5/8" x 7 5/8")

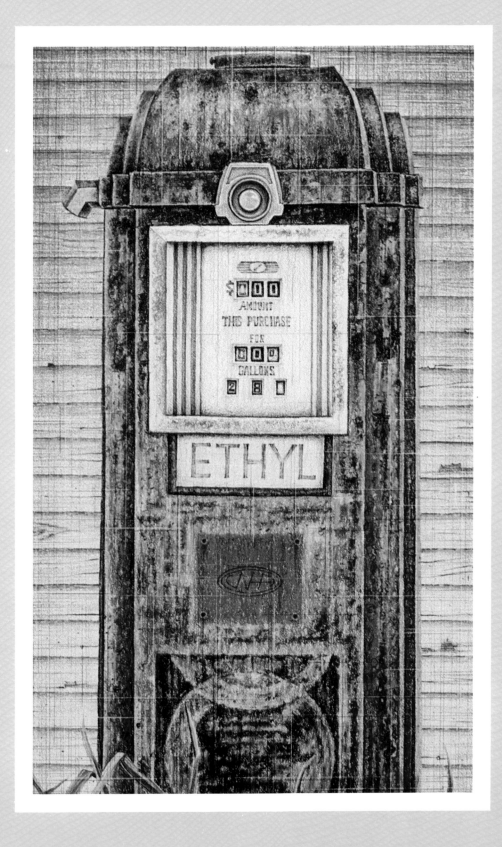

Continuing Attractions

Although they were not intended as a beacon to the itinerant traveler, the movie theatre signs that emerged in the 1920s and 1930s are clearly on a scale that can attract the eye of the motorist. But within these large signs there is frequently a great deal of intricate detail worthy of close-up sustained perusal. So even though these marquees and signs might attract the attention of a person in a moving car a block away, that same person, as a pedestrian, can also feast on the details from a distance of a few feet. Thus, like other masterpieces, these ornate street-side art forms are worthy of aesthetic contemplation. Moreover, on nearly every Main Street of any American town of over two thousand population these brightly illuminated theatre signs were in their heyday, a focal point of another kind; they provided a sense of community. This feeling prevailed along the older business thoroughfares until the automobile stretched them to the extent that they were attenuated by outlying shopping centers.

In both smaller towns and larger cities, many of these entertainment palaces have closed. The ones that survive, however, continue to be streetside attractions. Yet even the derelict sign of the closed theatre carries on the show in its own way. And all bespeak a level of artistry no longer practical for the outside of a movie house.

Embodied in those marquees that remain is an implicit "Hurray-for-Hollywood" attitude. On many Main Streets this is but a faint echo from the era when an escape to the movies was a wondrous event. The outside of the movie palace was consistent with what was offered on the inside. There was more sparkle than despair. Perhaps even those palaces that are now closed could turn their signs back on to rekindle some of those feelings. For now let these drawings work toward that possibility.

Fox Aglow in Westwood

Los Angeles, California

Late-1920s photographs of this area near the UCLA campus reveal a relatively sparsely settled landscape containing a movie theatre, its tower dominating the skyline. The same tower still serves as a perpetual beacon, announcing an ongoing Hollywood premiere. Its contours and decoration are in the spirit of the Baroque movie palaces of this era. The letters, though not yet evolved into the more rotund cookie-cutter shapes, carry a hint of the emerging Moderne style. The drawing shows a peeling patina and a wing askew, implying a dereliction that in this case is inconsistent with the theatre's thriving business. It is still at its pinnacle after over a half century. But because this sign is itself a pinnacle it is apparently not too accessible. One has to climb a long way to screw in a light bulb. Incidentally that very appropriate technicolor sky does occasionally occur in the Los Angeles area. Once again life imitates art. *(115/8" x 75/8")*

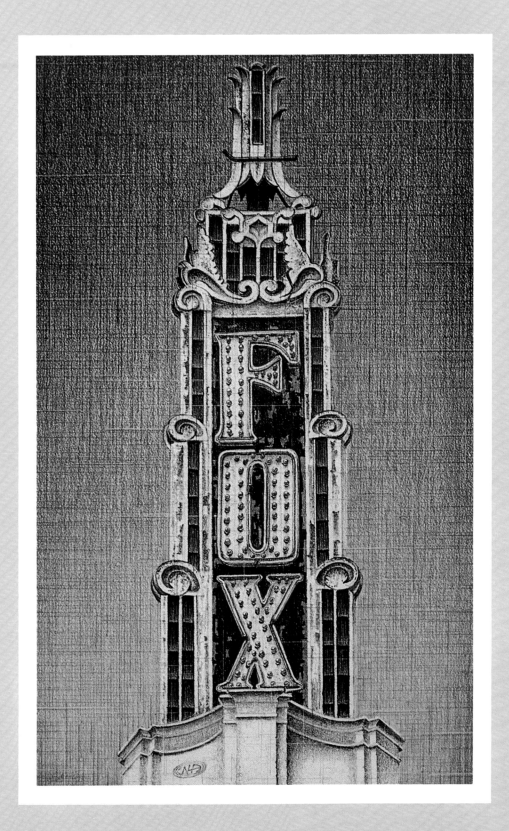

Moderne Royalty on Wilshire

Los Angeles, California

In the twenties Wilshire Boulevard began to evolve as a motorist-oriented shopping strip west of downtown Los Angeles. Stores were designed with main entrances at the rear facing large parking lots for these motorized consumers. What emerged was a ready-made auto-age Main Street. And, along this new mercantile route, some theatres were built. This Spanish king occupies a streamlined palace with a soaring facade. The building itself is in character with the World's Fair architecture of the 1930s. The ornate sign, by harmonious contrast, retains more Baroque treatments in its fanciful neon. The letter *E* at the top and the *R* further down make an excellent transition between the differing styles of the sign and the facade. And of course the name of the theatre is also somewhat transitional—a bit of Español along Anglo Wilshire, well west of the original site of the Spanish settlement established in 1781. (*11 5/8" x 7 5/8"*)

Foxed Out in Tucson

Tucson, Arizona

For nearly four decades the show went on inside this establishment and in three other theatres along Congress Street in downtown Tucson. The Fox theatre, though closed, is the sole intact survivor of movie palace days along this former major east-west business thoroughfare. Two of its three contemporaries have actually been torn down. Its own status is tenuous. For now it comprises a time capsule of the past.

It is, however, a mixed time capsule. Though it opened in the mid 1930s, its Zigzag Moderne facade, with the stylized floral motif, dates back to the 1920s. The letters of the sign tend toward the Streamlined Modern style of the thirties themselves. The scrollwork and the accompanying light bulbs are in more of the Baroque movie palace style. To put it gently, the old Fox is somewhat eclectic. So, though the show no longer goes on inside, this theatre still offers a glimmer of its former spectacle. May it continue to elude the ongoing hunt of the wrecking crews and those who sponsor them. (*11 5/8" x 7 5/8"*)

All American Grilles Along the Way

The roadside objects depicted in this section are even more ephemeral than those portrayed thus far. Mostly they appear on the outskirts of small towns. Their habitat is what was once referred to as a junk yard. Now it is a salvage yard. Beyond this shift in language use there also resides in these places some automotive vestiges that are of considerable artistic interest—the more ornately adorned vehicles of the 1950s. Their flair is in keeping with many of the other roadside forms of that era and those immediately preceding. This flair, a kind of technological panache, is most evident in the grilles of the vehicles of that time.

The very idea of a grille, as a skin over a functional radiator, shows a shift in consciousness from raw function to a kind of aestheticism. Though some did cleave the wind, they were mainly decorative. And what decoration they were. Like their roadside counterparts they spoke with individuality with regard to their makers. Each make of automobile could be readily distinguished from another. Each had a personality of its own. Some were stately, others funny. True, there was a glut of chrome on the more flamboyant models. But it was a well crafted bit of shining artistry up front. It was somewhat given to excess. This excess was coupled with zest, something lacking in their meager successors. Efficiency has won over aesthetics. There must be a way of combining both. For now, let this limited sampling of drawings suffice.

Derelict DeSoto

Hernando DeSoto neither invented this car nor consented to the use of his name on it. (Of course, Chief Pontiac was not consulted about the use of his name for that marque either.) The grilles of those DeSotos of the 1950s that still survive reign as monuments to a time when art and engineering merged to give us a sculpture that intuitively seemed bent on celebrating the Eisenhower era of automotive opulence. These chrome masterpieces of the fifties provide quite a different metaphor from that of their dinky look-alike rectangular counterparts of the present. (11 5/8" x 7 5/8")

Marilyn Monroe Caddy

To be exact, this drawing is of a 1956 Cadillac. It is typical of the front-end ornamentation of that time. Though Cadillacs were more expensive than most cars, even on less costly models the grilles were nearly as ornate and massive as this one. This grille achieves a little extra class by way of the gold finish on part of the emblem and on the interior of the grille. The rest of it is of the more typical chrome. It is the latter that provides a reflective interplay of many of the front-end features. Note the reflection of the headlight in one of the prominent protrusions. The sexist title does not necessarily reflect the artist's sensibilities. In those more naive times it seemed to be an apt nickname for an automobile with these anatomical features. Just another state of mind along the way. (*11 5/8" x 7 5/8"*)

Fin (115/8″ x 75/8″)